MW01098500

AARON SHEARER

Learning the Classic Guitar Part 3: Interpretation and Performance Development

edited by Tom Poore

CD CONTENTS

Guitarist - David Franzen
Recorded at New Horizons Studio, Kernersville, N.C.

© 1991 BY MEL BAY PUBLICATIONS, INC., PACIFIC, MO 63069.
ALL RIGHTS RESERVED. INTERNATIONAL COPYRIGHT SECURED. B.M.I. MADE AND PRINTED IN U.S.A.

Visit us on the Web at http://www.melbay.com — E-mail us at email@melbay.com

1 2 3 4 5 6 7 8 9 0

Contents

Interpretation

Performance Development

Preface

Although at first it may appear that interpretation and performance development have little in common, they're actually very closely linked. First, they're the only areas of guitar study which center upon the emotional aspects of playing music: In interpretation, students must learn to organize and convey to the listener their emotional response to music — in performance development, they must learn to deal positively with the excitement of playing for others. Further, both interpretation and performance require a secure foundation in technique, reading music, and memorization.

But there's another more subtle yet important similarity. By the time students learn to play short pieces with confidence and security, they've acquired the habit of concentrating mainly on the mechanical aspects of playing. *Both interpretation and performance, however, require an entirely different focus of concentration.* Students who are learning to interpret and perform music should no longer be concerned with technique, reading music, or memorization. Instead, they must learn to concentrate on the music itself.

As in all other areas of guitar study, students will progress more quickly and easily in interpretation and performance development if they're provided with secure basic concepts. Once these concepts become habitual, each student will then have a foundation of confidence from which to share the warmth of his or her personality with others. Thus, interpreting and performing music are the ultimate rewards for patient, diligent, and well-directed study.

Aaron Shearer
Winston-Salem, N.C.

Interpretation

Introduction

Among all the areas of guitar study, interpretation stands apart. Perhaps no other subject in music is so clouded in mystique. Interpretation is often seen as an entirely intuitive process — indeed, more than a few musicians would question whether anything of real value can be written about interpretation.

In view of this situation, it's essential to state the premise behind the interpretive approach in this book: *The most effective musical expression grows from rational organization.*

The accuracy of this premise is demonstrated on the recording which accompanies this book. Listen to the first musical example, in which Fernando Sor's "Andante" Op. 60, No. 14 is performed three times. (You'll find the score for this piece on p. 53.):

1) In the first performance, the guitarist has tried to play the music exactly as written — his intent was to add nothing beyond what the composer notated in the score. But although this performance adheres to the letter of the score, it sounds stiff and lifeless. Such a performance would be unacceptable to a sensitive listener.

2) In the second performance, the guitarist has added life and spirit to the music through rhythmic and dynamic nuances. *But notice how disorganized and ineffective this performance sounds.* Indeed, any guitarist who played music in this manner would be dismissed as an erratic and insensitive interpreter.

3) In the third performance, the guitarist has again used rhythmic and dynamic nuances to add life and spirit to the music. But notice how much more effective it is compared to the second performance. It displays more balance and proportion — in a word, it's better *organized.*

Admittedly, the second performance is a deliberate distortion of the music. But this only reinforces our premise. Since we can distinguish between good and bad performances, we obviously expect expression to be organized in certain basic ways.

The importance of organization in expressive playing doesn't diminish the importance of intuition. Intuition will always be an essential part of expression. Within the organization of expression there are many possibilities — ultimately, the decision about how to use them is yours and yours alone. Further, many of the more refined aspects of expression can never be fully organized.

But as an interpreter, it's insufficient for you to rely on intuition alone. An effective interpretation generally conveys an overall sense of balance and proportion, and these qualities are most fully achieved through organization. Thus, you must learn how to organize your intuitive ideas effectively. The more accurately and confidently you can do this, the more expressively you'll be able to interpret music.

Of course, no book can fully explain interpretation. Careful listening — hearing how other musicians apply expression — is an essential part of your study. Further, much of your development will come through the *act* of interpreting music — learning to move and shape music according to your sense of balance, proportion, and refinement. But listening and practicing are useful only to the extent that you have clear concepts to guide you. To learn through listening, you need concepts which enable you to competently evaluate a performance. To practice most efficiently, you need concepts which provide you with clear aims.

Approaching Expressive Interpretation

Perhaps no aspect of music receives more attention than interpretation. As we saw in the introduction, the same piece, depending on how it's interpreted, can be either lifeless and boring or vital and interesting. Interpretation is so powerful that it can sway our evaluation of the music itself — we may find an expressive interpretation of a mediocre piece more appealing than an inexpressive interpretation of a superb piece.

Before proceeding, the terms "interpretation" and "expression" need to be clarified:

- *Interpretation* refers to the playing of a composition — it's the result of the performer's concept of how the composition should be played and his or her ability to realize this concept.

- *Expression* refers to all the qualities — either found in the score or provided by the performer — which give life and feeling to music. Thus, an interpretation can be either more or less expressive, depending on the quality of the music and the skill of the performer.

Expression can be divided into two categories:

1) *Compositional expression* refers to the expressive qualities which can be found in a score. This includes rhythm, pitch, and harmony — it may also include indications of dynamics and timbre, and even basic descriptions of mood and spirit. The expressive qualities found in any particular score are influenced by the following factors:

a. The historical period in which the score was composed — for example, the range of compositional expression available to 19th century Romantic composers was greater than the range available to 17th century Baroque composers.

b. The quality of the composition itself — the better the composition, the greater its expressive content.

c. The relative amount of expressive indications supplied by the composer — one composer may use many dynamic markings, while another may use few or none.

2) *Interpretive expression* refers to nuance, inflection, and all the other qualities which are contributed by the performer. Performers begin, of course, with the expressive materials found in the score, so there's some overlap between interpretive and compositional expression. But performers also go beyond, adding expressive qualities which can't be found in the score.

∞   ∞   ∞   ∞   ∞   ∞   ∞

Our main concern is with interpretive expression. For the sake of brevity, this book will often use the term "expression" when referring to interpretive expression.

The Expressive Musician

Expression cannot be entirely planned before a performance. You can form general ideas which will guide you while playing, and you can even plan to interpret specific passages in a certain way. But the nuances of an expressive interpretation are too elusive to be precisely planned and carried out. Rather, you must develop the ability to improvise expression, responding artistically to the music as you play.

A good analogy for how well-trained musicians approach expression is the way in which skilled actors approach performing. Like musicians, actors work from a "score" — in their case, a script. And like musicians, actors must bring the script to life—in their case, largely through vocal nuance, inflection, and cadence.

As they speak, skilled actors aren't thinking about the elements of language — grammar, words, syllables, and punctuation. Nor are they consciously planning every nuance and inflection of these elements. Rather, through years of intensive training, they've polished their expressive command of speech to a high degree. They're acutely aware of how cadence, nuance, and inflection affect their listeners. Thus, skilled actors have cultivated the ability to *improvise* expression as they speak — responding to the script in ways that deeply impress the audience.

Expressive musicians perform in a similar way. They've polished their intuitive command of expression to a high degree. Through careful study and practice, they've become sensitive to the way expression touches our emotions. *Thus, well-trained musicians have cultivated the ability to improvise expression as they perform, responding to music in ways that are both aesthetically appealing and moving to the audience.*

∾ ∾ ∾ ∾ ∾ ∾ ∾

Because expression must be improvised, it can never be fixed. Thus, there can never be a "definitive interpretation." Each interpretation creates its own mood and environment, and it will succeed or fail on its own merits.

Well-trained concert musicians understand the elusive nature of expression. They realize that one performance may be especially moving, while another may be relatively less so. But, having attained confidence in their expressive abilities, they expect that every performance they give will be satisfying to their listeners.

Expression and Technique

Many of us have heard a performance in which the notes were played cleanly and accurately, but with little feeling or spirit. While we may admire the skill behind it, such a performance has little power to touch our emotions.

For the expressive musician, technical study is a starting point — it's the necessary preparation for acquiring the skills needed to play expressively. Musicians with inadequate technique lack the freedom to pursue their expressive ideas. Further, listeners won't be moved if they're constantly distracted by a musician's technical deficiencies.

But technique can never be more than a means for conveying expression. Ultimately, the technique required for expressive nuance and inflection grows only from the pursuit of expression. Indeed, it's the pursuit of expression which refines technique to its highest level.

Regarding Early Music

Although we can never know exactly how expression has changed over the past five centuries, the basic way music touches our emotions seems to be constant. The rhythmic patterns and melodic and harmonic contrasts in early music still appeal to us today.

Consider, for example, the well-known Pavanes by Luis Milan, published in 1536. The qualities in Milan's music that stir our emotions must have similarly touched those who heard it in 1536. We can assume that listeners have always responded in a similar way throughout all periods of music. Thus, the study of expression applies equally well to early music.

Since early music occupies a prominent role in the guitar repertoire, you may wish to become familiar with historical performance practices. A particularly useful source is Thurston Dart's *The Interpretation of Music* (Harper and Row, New York and Evanston, 1963). It also contains an extensive bibliography for further reference.

The Basis of Expressive Playing: Enhancing and Creating Musical Contrast

Contrast pervades our lives. From the moment we're born, we experience the life-sustaining contrasts between instability and stability. Our first gasp for breath is an instinctive response to the discomfort caused by our body's need for oxygen. Each breath produces a moment of relative stability before we once again respond to our need for more oxygen. We respond to the discomfort of hunger by eating, to the discomfort of fatigue by resting, and so on. These are the natural contrasts we respond to in order to exist.

But we're not satisfied with merely responding to these natural contrasts. The human mind is restless and quickly subject to boredom — it finds mere existence unacceptable. Thus, we enhance the contrasts necessary for existence by creating our own additional contrasts. Eating, for example, becomes more than a basic act of sustenance — by adding variety and refinement, we make it a more interesting and pleasurable experience.

Indeed, our need for contrast is so great that we go beyond simply enhancing the contrasts necessary for existence. We also create contrasts for their own sake. For example, an evening at the theater or socializing with good friends becomes a pleasant contrast to our daily routine. These contrasts are unrelated to mere existence — rather, they're the contrasts which add diversity and excitement to our lives. They give our lives a uniquely human meaning.

And so it is in music. The score, of course, consists of written musical contrasts. But a mere mechanical reproduction of these contrasts would be unacceptable to any sensitive listener. To be expressive, musical contrasts must be enhanced in a sensitive, refined, and life-like manner. Further, to heighten the effectiveness of their performances, expressive musicians create contrasts beyond those which can be found in the score.

Enhancing and creating musical contrast is the most important issue in expressive playing — it's the essence of how performers bring music to life. To expressive performers, every contrast in the score — be it a rise or fall in pitch, or a change in rhythm or harmony — is an opportunity for interpretive expression. Further, to add mood and spirit to the music, expressive performers also create contrasts beyond those which can be found in the score.

Expression and the Score

The musical score is more than a set of instructions that tells you what notes to play. It's a blueprint of a living piece of music. The score is our best link — in most cases, our only link — to the composer's expressive intentions. Even the most mechanical interpretation of the score will convey some degree of expression. Thus, all expression begins with the score.

There are, however, limits to what the score can tell us in terms of expression:

- **It's impossible to adequately notate the full range of expressive variations which are possible in rhythm, pitch, dynamics, and timbre.**

- **It's impossible to list every nuance and inflection that goes into an expressive performance. For example, an expressive performance requires almost constant subtle rhythmic fluctuations — it would be futile for a composer to try to notate all these fluctuations.**

But these apparent limitations are actually strengths. Because the subtleties of expression can't be precisely notated, we're not limited to a fixed manner of expression. The score provides for individuality. In a sense then, musical notation is the perfect medium for this living, varying art.

This is another way in which music is similar to drama. Vocal nuance, inflection, and cadence — crucial to an effective dramatic performance — can't be written into a script. To become an eloquent interpreter, an actor must learn to recognize the emotional potential of the script. Like the script, the full expressive potential of a musical score can only be realized through the performer. To a well-trained musician, the score is a rich source of expressive potential. Indeed, a fine performer can create expressive qualities which even the composer may never have imagined.[†]

∞　　∞　　∞　　∞　　∞　　∞　　∞

Initially, of course, your efforts in learning the guitar have been directed toward playing with acceptable accuracy and tone. This is a necessary stage of your development — since expression focuses largely on the score, the study of expression must be deferred until you acquire the skills needed to play short pieces. Now, assuming that you've acquired these skills, you're ready to begin exploring the expressive potential of a score.

A score's expressive potential is directly related to the ability of the performer who reads it. You must learn to recognize this expressive potential. You'll begin by examining one of the most basic of expressive materials that can be found in the score: melodic contour.

Beginning to Play Expressively: Observing Melodic Contour

When approaching a piece, you should begin by considering the contrasts in pitch and rhythm found in the melody. Every melody has its own unique shape or outline, which is called the *melodic contour*. A melody's contour can reveal much about how expression should be applied.

An easy way to begin understanding how melodic contour can influence expression is through the simple visual imagery which follows. (Generally, a metronome shouldn't be used during this procedure — it would tend to restrict your flexibility with the melody.)

[†]Perceptive composers are aware of this. A concert pianist once asked Aaron Copland if he had any advice on how to interpret his "Piano Variations." Replied Copland, "Surprise me."

Hiking the Mountain Range (See Ex. 1, p. 13):

Notice the mountain-range skyline which has been drawn to conform to the melodic contour of Ex. 1.[†] We'll visualize ourselves hiking a mountain trail which follows the ridge of the skyline:

• It takes more energy to hike up a mountain, so follow your tendency to increase the energy and excitement by playing gradually louder as you ascend. It takes less energy to hike down a mountain, so you should indicate this by playing gradually softer as you descend.

• From our trailhead at So (measure 1), we gradually climb toward the peak at Re.[††] On reaching Re, we find that there isn't a good place to rest, so we continue onward. Now we descend briefly into a small gully (Do, Ti). Almost immediately we climb back to Do (measure 4), a half note, which gives us time for a brief rest.

• After resting, we ascend to another Re and discover a level section of trail along this high ridge (measure 5). Soon the trail begins to descend and continues down to So (measure 8) — the same elevation at which we began our hike. This half note marks the halfway point in our hike, so we stop for lunch and a rest.

• After a pleasant rest, we prepare to continue our hike. The melodic contour shows that we'll begin with a sharp climb to Re (measure 9). This isn't too difficult, since a resting place along the way (the eighth rest) gives us time to catch our breath.

[†]This is "Scale Song" (Duet No. 10) from *Part Two*, p. 26.
[††]For an explanation of solfege syllables, see *Part Two*, pp. 209–211.

- On reaching the summit, we're glad to find another level section of trail before descending rather sharply to Ti (measure 10). We take another short rest before making a brief descent to La, where we continue along another level stretch of trail. This is followed by a sharp climb to Do, followed by a gradual ascent back to Re (measure 13). It's late afternoon now, and we're happy to see that our trail leads downward, all the way back to So.

- After an enjoyable hike we stop and rest at the trail's end, recalling the beauty we encountered along the way.

Now try this with the guitar. Remember, play gradually louder as you ascend and gradually softer as you descend — in relatively level passages, maintain an even dynamic level.

Scale Song

Ex. 1

S-H

14

This approach to beginning expression is also effective in solos consisting of a melody and a bass. The following solo, "Serenade I," is the first such piece to be found in *Part Two*. Notice again the skyline drawn to conform to the contour of the melody — you should play gradually louder as you ascend and gradually softer as you descend.

As you carry out this approach with "Serenade I," bear in mind that the basses are only an accompaniment. Thus, they need only conform to the dynamic contrasts of the melody.

Serenade I

Ex. 2

A. S.

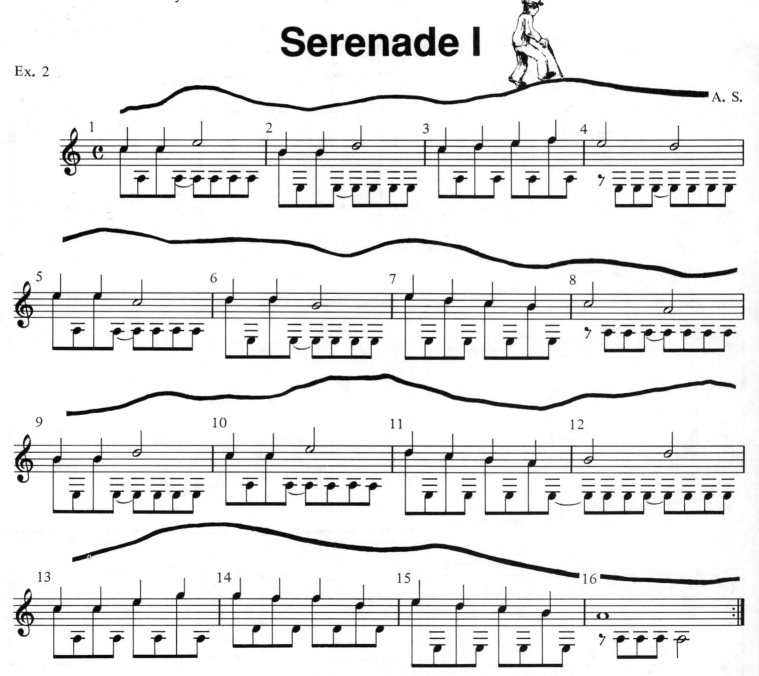

At this point, you're learning to recognize and expressively respond to contrasts within the *overall* melodic contour. Thus, be flexible as you use this procedure with other melodies, and don't be concerned about details of a melodic contour that don't exactly conform to the mountain-range image.

This, of course, is only an introduction to expressive playing. You've begun with a modest hike through the musical terrain, acquiring a general feel for how melodic contour influences expression. As you become adept with this manner of applying expression, however, you'll be ready to approach musical contrast in a more creative manner. By looking more closely at music, you'll soon discover a world of beauty normally hidden from the untrained eye and ear.

To the teacher: How long and to what extent this procedure proves beneficial will depend on the individual student. You may find that some students respond better to more detailed imagery of the hike. Also, this procedure can be used to introduce more sophisticated expression — perhaps even including rubato.

The Moving and Shaping Forces of Music

Sound powerfully influences our lives. Disturbing and ominous sounds arouse us — agreeable sounds soothe us. Sounds in music affect us in a similar way. Harsh, loud, irregular, rapid, and dissonant sounds leaping up and down in pitch excite our emotions. Mellow, soft, regular, slow-moving, and consonant sounds on an even pitch level calm our emotions. Contrasts between these qualities create what is sensed as *activity* and *rest*.

Activity and rest are formed through the five basic materials of music:

- **RHYTHM: Activity is created through contrasting note values and rhythmic patterns, and through quick movement and tempo. Rest is created through unchanging note values and rhythmic patterns, evenly spaced beats, and slow movement and tempo.**

- **MELODY: Activity and rest are created by the relative contrasts between successive pitches. Whether a change in pitch creates activity or rest depends on how it's affected by the other four materials of music.**

- **HARMONY: In tonal music, activity and rest are created through the contrast between an unstable harmony and its resolution. In atonal music, activity and rest are created through the progression of harmonies, implying the contrast between stability and instability.**

- **DYNAMICS AND TIMBRE: Contrasting dynamic levels and shades of timbre contribute activity and rest — they also intensify the effects of harmony, melody, and rhythm.**

∾ ∾ ∾ ∾ ∾ ∾ ∾

Activity and rest are essential moving and shaping forces of music. But they alone don't provide sufficient direction for performing music expressively. To play music expressively, the performer must organize the contrasting forces of activity and rest in a way which appeals to the listener.

Attractions

Attractions are the basic organizing forces of music — they impart a logical and aesthetic coherence to music. Thus, attractions are powerful moving and shaping forces — they're the means through which a performer begins to expressively organize musical contrasts.

Attraction is the tendency of certain tones to gravitate toward successive tones. Although this implies that sound has an intrinsic ability to pull on other sounds, this is not the case — attraction occurs only in the listener's ear. For example, when you hear the sequence Do, Re, Mi, Fa, So, La, Ti, you next expect to hear Do. If the next sound isn't Do, you experience instability and tension. Of course, the next sound may not be Do, and that can be a nice surprise — providing that the music eventually returns to Do.

When music conveys instability, the ear instinctively seeks stability. Even the most dissonant music must have an appealing blend of relative stability (rest) and instability (activity). Without this blend of emotional tension and release, music contradicts our deepest natural drives and sensibilities.

There are three kinds of attractions:[†]

1) rhythmic attraction
2) melodic attraction
3) harmonic attraction

Because rhythm sets all other musical forces in motion, rhythmic attraction is the most powerful of the three kinds of attractions. Thus, we'll begin by examining rhythmic attraction.

[†]See Diran Alexanian's *Interpretation Musicale et Instrumentale, Six Suites pour Violoncelle seul, J. S. Bach*, Editions Salebert, 22 rue Chachat, Paris.

Rhythmic Attraction

Rhythmic attraction creates a sense of momentum and arrival between two or more successive tones. There are two kinds of rhythmic attraction:

1) ATTRACTION BY DURATION: Among notes of short and long duration, shorter notes are normally attracted to a successive note of longer duration.

Curved lines (called "slurs") are commonly used to indicate the grouping of notes. Using the neutral syllable "tah," sing the following examples, carefully connecting the group of notes within each slur. Notice that, through the momentum of the shorter notes, you tend to accent the longer note.

Ex. 3

2) ATTRACTION OF THE STRONG BEAT: Among notes of equal duration, notes which fall on weak beats are normally attracted to a note which falls on the strong beat. The *metric pulse* (the first beat of each measure) is always a strong beat.

In $\frac{2}{4}$, the second beat is weak:

Ex. 4

In $\frac{3}{4}$, both the second and third beats are weak. Thus, depending on the musical context, $\frac{3}{4}$ can be grouped in either of the following ways:

Ex. 5

In $\frac{4}{4}$ ($\frac{2}{4}+\frac{2}{4}$), beats one and three are strong; beats two and four are weak:

Ex. 6

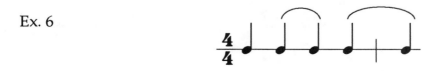

In applying attraction of the strong beat, the faster the tempo, the longer can be the note value which defines the beat — the slower the tempo, the shorter can be the note value which defines the beat.

For example, at slower tempos, a beat which normally falls on a longer value can be subdivided so that it falls on a note of shorter value. Consider the following:

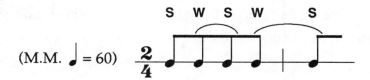

Although the meter is $\frac{2}{4}$, the tempo is slow enough so that the eighth notes can be treated as alternating strong and weak beats. This means that attraction of the strong beat now applies between pairs of eighth notes. At an even slower tempo, attraction of the strong beat can apply between pairs of sixteenth notes. *Thus, the slower the tempo, the more opportunity you have for expressively grouping notes of shorter value.*

Melodic Attraction

Melodic attraction is based on the relative attraction between successive pitches in scales and arpeggios.

In scalewise movement, the strength of melodic attraction depends on three factors:

1) how firmly a sense of "key" is established
2) how clearly the direction of movement is felt
3) the position of the tones within the scale

Once the key is established through a clear direction of scalewise tones, the attraction of successive tones is strong. For example, in solfeging an ascending C-major scale (see Ex. 7), at approximately midway through the scale you'll begin to feel the attraction of the higher Do. Indeed, each tone seems to be attracted to the next successive tone — the closer you get to Do, the stronger the attraction. A similar attraction occurs when the scale is descending.

Ex. 7

Almost any stepwise progression of tones can result in melodic attraction. Ex. 8a illustrates successive tones which change direction — Ex. 8b illustrates an immediate stepwise movement in the opposite direction following a leap:

Ex. 8a   Ex. 8b

Tones of the same duration which appear as an arpeggio within a melodic context generally result in melodic attraction:

Ex. 9

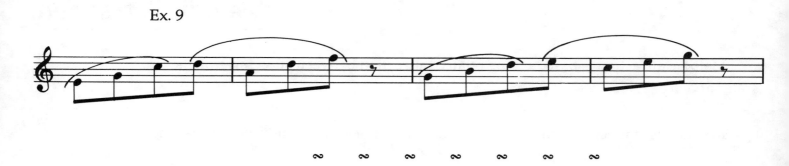

Grouping is rarely based exclusively on melodic attraction. Indeed, melodic attraction is strongest when it occurs in conjunction with harmonic attraction, rhythmic attraction, or both.

Harmonic Attraction

In tonal music, harmonic attraction is the gravitation of *unstable harmonies* (active) to *stable harmonies* (restful). The primary force behind harmonic attraction is the activity or rest which exists between simultaneously sounding pitches — this accounts for the tendency of certain chords to gravitate toward successive chords.

Ex. 10

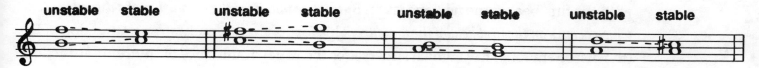

Ex. 11 shows how melody often functions in conjunction with harmony, where the upper note of each chord is melodic and the lower notes form the harmony.

Ex. 11

There are instances, however, when melodic activity is minimal and harmonic attraction predominates:

Ex. 12

Although rhythmic attraction is generally recognized as the most powerful attraction in expression, both melodic and harmonic attraction can occasionally overshadow its usual dominance. For example:

Ex. 13

According to rhythmic attraction, the Ti in measure 2 would normally be grouped with the first beat of the next measure. *But notice that Ti is the resolution of a dissonant tone which occurs on the first beat of the measure.* This forms an extremely strong attraction of Do (the dissonant tone) to Ti which supersedes the usual dominance of rhythmic attraction. Thus, the Ti in measure 2 must be grouped with the preceding Do. (A similar situation exists in measure 4.)[†]

Although the environment in atonal music is radically different, both melodic and harmonic attraction can still exist. Once a particular environment of activity and rest has been established, tones or harmonies sensed to be unstable will be attracted to those sensed to be more stable.

Ex. 14

[†]To thoroughly understand both melodic and harmonic attraction, you need a working knowledge of music theory — a subject beyond the scope of this book. If you haven't already done so, you should begin studying theory with a good teacher as soon as possible. A background in music theory makes all areas of music more meaningful and easier to understand.

Organizing Rhythmic Contrasts: Note-Grouping and Phrasing

With an understanding of the moving and shaping forces of music, you now have the means to approach expression in a more effective manner. Note-grouping and phrasing are the syntax of expression — they're the means through which music gains expressive shape and structure.

Note-grouping and phrasing are based mainly on rhythmic attraction.[†] Thus, you'll now begin to expressively organize the rhythmic contrasts in music.

To define note-grouping and phrasing accurately, you first need a clear understanding of the musical phrase, its content, and how it is formed. You'll begin with the basic constituent of a phrase: the figure.

The Figure

A *figure*[††] consists of two or more notes which are related to each other by attraction — it's the smallest musically coherent group of notes. A figure often consists of only two or three notes, but more notes may be included if they are played rapidly enough for rhythmic attraction to occur:

Ex. 15

[†]Remember, however, that melodic and harmonic attraction can occasionally overshadow the usual dominance of rhythmic attraction.
[††]Musicians sometimes use the terms "motive" (or motif) and "figure" synonymously. But, since "motive" usually has thematic implications, "figure" more accurately serves our purpose. A figure becomes a motive only when it recurs throughout a composition.

A note which isn't part of a figure is a *rhythmic syllable*. For example, notice that the half notes in the first two measures of Ex. 16 aren't preceded by notes of shorter value. Thus, since these notes aren't part of a figure, they're rhythmic syllables:

Ex. 16

There are two kinds of figures: those which begin on a weak beat, and those which begin on a strong beat. A figure which begins on a weak beat is an *upbeat figure:*

Ex. 17

A. In duple meter, an upbeat figure begins on the second beat:

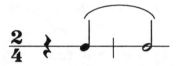

B. In triple meter, an upbeat figure begins on either the second or third beat:

C. In quadruple meter, an upbeat figure begins on either the second or fourth beat:

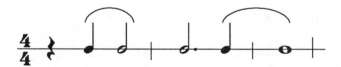

A figure which begins on a strong beat is a *downbeat figure:*

Ex. 18

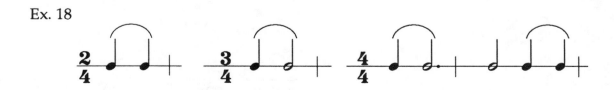

Both upbeat and downbeat figures are based on rhythmic attraction.

The Phrase

A *phrase* is a more or less unified group of figures or figures and rhythmic syllables which results in either a pause or a conclusion:

Ex. 19

There are two distinct forms of phrases:

• *Dialogue phrase:* A dialogue phrase consists of two consecutive groups of figures or figures and rhythmic syllables which give the impression of balancing each other. The first part of the dialogue phrase, called the *antecedent,* is a short musical statement which doesn't effectively stand alone — thus, it seems to invite a response. An antecedent is marked by a brief pause or breath. The second part, called the *consequent,* is another short statement in response to the antecedent. Together, the antecedent and consequent give a feeling of proportion — that a more or less balanced statement and response has occurred.

The following rhythmic example is a short dialogue phrase — the first three-note group is answered by an identical group:

Ex. 20

• *Continuous phrase:* A continuous phrase consists of an unbroken succession of figures which continues without significant pause to the end of the phrase. It gives the feeling that a more or less complete statement has been made, and concludes with varying degrees of finality, marked by a pause or breath.

The following rhythmic example is a continuous phrase — it contains no distinctive pause to indicate a separation into an antecedent and consequent:

Ex. 21

Defining Note-Grouping and Phrasing

The preceding information now provides a basis for defining note-grouping and phrasing:

- **Note-grouping is the act of expressively grouping notes either to enhance a figure which is indicated in the score or to create a figure where none is indicated.**

- **Phrasing is the act of expressively grouping figures — or figures and rhythmic syllables — either to form a phrase which is indicated in the score or to create a phrase where none is indicated.[†]**

Notice that both note-grouping and phrasing are *acts* of expressive grouping. Although figures and phrases can be indicated in the score, only the performer can expressively convey them. Composers can indicate where certain figures and phrases begin and end, but they can't describe what must occur expressively from note to note within a figure or from figure to figure within a phrase. Thus, note-grouping and phrasing always refer to the expressive contribution of the performer, whether the performer is enhancing the figures and phrases indicated in the score or creating additional figures and phrases which aren't indicated in the score.

∞ ∞ ∞ ∞ ∞ ∞ ∞

The most effective manner of note-grouping and phrasing centers on activity brought about by the subtle alteration of rhythm — commonly called "rubato."

[†]Some musicians use "phrasing" to describe the expressive grouping of notes into figures. But this often proves confusing to students — since "phrasing" refers to the phrase, it seems illogical to use this term also to refer to the grouping of notes into a figure. Thus, for the purposes of this book, "phrasing" will refer only to the act of organizing figures into phrases. The expressive grouping of notes into a figure will be referred to as "note-grouping."

Rubato

Rubato is the intentional varying of the durations of tones and silences from their written values. These variations cause subtle rhythmic fluctuations within figures, phrases, and even the overall tempo.

> More than any other expressive element, rubato gives life and movement to music. Rubato is the most powerful and effective means of expression — indeed, it's through rubato that note-grouping and phrasing are born.

Although effective rubato involves feeling and intuition, it doesn't imply whimsical or aimless tempo fluctuations.[†] Without a clear knowledge of note-grouping and phrasing, performers often apply meaningless or inappropriate rubato — slackening the pace when movement is clearly needed, or vice versa. To use rubato effectively, the performer must have definite intentions of rhythmic pace and movement.

Rubato is generally most effective when a relatively secure pulse is maintained. A clear metric pulse gives the listener a feeling of order and stability — rubato passages provide an appealing contrast of fluidity and movement. If the metric pulse isn't relatively secure, orderly contrast is lessened and the effect of rubato is greatly reduced.

Traditionally, rubato is often explained as the robbing of time from one or more notes which is then repaid to successive notes. (Indeed, the Italian meaning of rubato is "robbed.") Certainly a performer can use rubato in approximately this way — slowing one passage, then proportionately rushing the next. But this traditional explanation of rubato can be misleading. It implies that you must calculate tempo fluctuations so that you arrive at the end of the composition at the same time you would have had you played in strict tempo. This is a mistaken idea. Rubato is not a mathematical exercise — rather, it's an effective way to impart flexibility, feeling, and spirit to music.

[†]Nor should rubato be confused with *ad libitum* (Latin, "at will"). This indication (generally abbreviated *ad lib.*) gives the performer freedom to alter the tempo at will — presumably within the limits of good taste.

Upbeat Grouping

Upbeat grouping is the subtle application of rubato either to enhance an upbeat figure which is indicated in the score or to create an upbeat figure where none is indicated. This is done by leaning a weak beat toward and smoothly connecting it with the successive strong beat. "Leaning" is done by slightly delaying the weak beat, and then rushing it to land on the strong beat precisely in tempo. Although the degree of delay can vary greatly — from almost imperceptible to clearly evident — when done effectively, the actual delay of the weak beat is usually very subtle.

Upbeat grouping creates vitality and contrast within the rhythmic framework. It also emphasizes the metric pulse in a subtle and aesthetically pleasing way.

Upbeat grouping is often indicated in the score. In each of the following examples, a long note on a strong beat is immediately preceded by a shorter note on a weak beat — this is both attraction by duration and attraction of the strong beat. Notice that your eye tends to group the short note with the following long note:

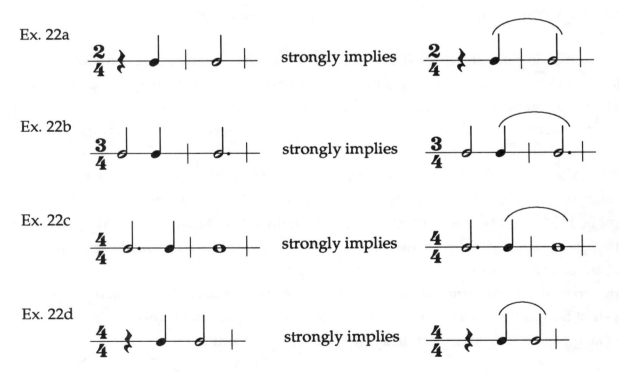

Listen to the recording of Exs. 23a and 23b, and then try playing them yourself. Count as you play, and group the weak beat with the strong downbeat:

Ex. 23a

Ex. 23b

The previous examples illustrate upbeat grouping which is indicated in the score. Often, however, it's not indicated in the score, yet it's still essential for an expressive rendition of the music. When upbeat grouping isn't indicated, its application is left entirely to the performer's discretion. The following sequence of examples explains an effective way of applying upbeat grouping in this situation.

Consider the following passage:

Ex. 24

Notice that nothing in this example suggests upbeat grouping. Indeed, the most obvious grouping of the passage is metric grouping, which is conveyed by simply accenting the first beat of each measure:

Ex. 25

In actual performance, however, metric grouping (simply accenting the metric pulse) soon becomes monotonous. To give Ex. 25 activity and life, you need to group it in a manner which creates contrast within the rhythmic framework.

An effective way to do this is through the subtle application of rubato, as demonstrated on the recording of Ex. 26. Notice the slight break between counts 2 and 3, and that count 3 leans slightly toward and connects with count 1 (the strong beat) of the following measure. Listen carefully, and then try it yourself.

Ex. 26

Notice that this provides an interesting interplay of two groupings within the rhythmic framework — a grouping which begins with the weak third beat...

Ex. 27a

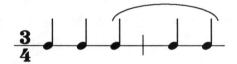

...which contrasts with the grouping provided by the metric pulse:

Ex. 27b

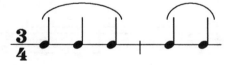

This avoids monotony and gives the passage activity and life.

Upbeat grouping[†] is equally effective in duple meter and quadruple meter:

Ex. 28a

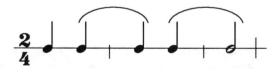

Ex. 28b

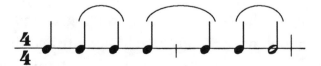

†For a scholarly and comprehensive explanation of upbeat grouping, see *Note-Grouping* by James Morgan Thurmond, published in 1982 by JMT Publications, P.O. Box 603/Camp Hill, PA 17011.

Downbeat Grouping

Downbeat grouping is the subtle application of rubato either to enhance a downbeat figure which is indicated in the score or to create a downbeat figure where none is indicated. This is done by slightly displacing a weak beat toward the preceding strong beat, causing the weak beat to be lengthened to slightly more than its written value. Emphasizing a weak beat creates a subtle feeling of rhythmic instability within the measure. *Bear in mind, however, that downbeat grouping requires a firm metric pulse to be most effective.*

Downbeat grouping is commonly used to provide a contrast to upbeat grouping. It's particularly effective in $\frac{3}{4}$ time — it makes the upbeat more active by interspersing a light accent on the weak second beat. Again, listen carefully to the recording and then practice the following:

Ex. 29

Like upbeat grouping, downbeat grouping can often be indicated in the score:

Ex. 30

 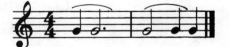

Summary

If your early attempts in expressive playing feel somewhat awkward, don't be discouraged. Like every other aspect of musical study, playing with refined and effective expression requires patient and well-directed study.

Always remember that the essence of expressive playing is its subtlety. Expression should appeal directly to the emotions — if your listeners become aware of the effort behind your expression, you're either overdoing it or doing it in the wrong way.

Questions for Review

Before continuing, you should be able to answer the following questions:

1. What is interpretation?
2. What is expression?
3. What is the single most important issue in expressive playing?
4. What are the five basic materials of music?
5. What are the moving and shaping forces of music?
6. What is attraction? What are the different kinds of attractions?
7. What is the smallest coherent group of notes in music? How many kinds are there?
8. What is a phrase? What are the two kinds of phrases?
9. What is note-grouping?
10. What is phrasing?
11. What is the most powerful means for creating expression?
12. What is rubato?
13. What are upbeat and downbeat grouping? Why are they important?

Answers

1. Interpretation refers to the playing of a composition — it's the result of the performer's concept of how the composition should be played and his or her ability to realize this concept.
2. Expression refers to all the qualities — either found in the score or provided by the performer — which give life and feeling to music.
3. Enhancing and creating musical contrast is the single most important issue in expressive playing.
4. The five basic materials of music are rhythm, melody, harmony, dynamics, and timbre.
5. The moving and shaping forces of music are activity and rest (formed through the five basic materials of music) and attractions.
6. Attraction is the tendency of certain tones to gravitate toward successive tones. Since sound has no intrinsic ability to pull on other sounds, attraction occurs only in the listener's ear. Attractions are the basic organizing forces of music. There are three kinds of attraction:

  a. Rhythmic attraction. (This is further divided into attraction by duration and attraction of the strong beat.)

  b. Melodic attraction.

  c. Harmonic attraction.

7. A figure is the smallest musically coherent group of successive notes found in music. There are two kinds of figures: those which begin on a weak beat, and those which begin on a strong beat. A figure which begins on a weak beat is an upbeat figure — this results in upbeat grouping. A figure which begins on a strong beat is a downbeat figure — this results in downbeat grouping.

8. A phrase is a more or less unified group of figures or figures and rhythmic syllables which results in either a pause or a conclusion. The two kinds of phrases are the dialogue phrase and the continuous phrase.

9. Note-grouping is the act of expressively grouping notes either to form a figure which is indicated in the score or to create a figure where none is indicated.

10. Phrasing is the act of expressively grouping figures — or figures and rhythmic syllables — either to form a phrase which is indicated in the score or to create a phrase where none is indicated.

11. Rubato is the most powerful means for creating expression.

12. Rubato is the intentional varying of the durations of tones and silences from their written values.

13. Upbeat grouping is the subtle application of rubato either to enhance an upbeat figure which is indicated in the score or to create an upbeat figure where none is indicated. This is done by slightly leaning a weak beat toward and smoothly connecting it with the successive strong beat.

Downbeat grouping is the subtle application of rubato either to enhance a downbeat figure which is indicated in the score or to create a downbeat figure where none is indicated. This is done by slightly displacing a weak beat toward the preceding strong beat, causing the weak beat to be lengthened to slightly more than its written value.

Both kinds of grouping are important because they create vitality and contrast within the rhythmic framework, giving activity and life to the music.

Approaching Expression through Vocalization

The most effective approach to learning the art of musical expression involves using your voice. Vocalization is the easiest and most natural way to feel note-grouping, and it tends to lead your fingers to a similar grouping on the guitar.

Vocalization refers to expressively using your voice in any of these three ways:

1) counting rhythms
2) singing solfege syllables
3) singing a neutral syllable ("lah" or "tah")

Ideally, you should sing the pitches accurately when vocalizing. If this is impractical, simply say the correct counting or solfege syllables while bending your voice to feel the melodic curve. Then vocalize the melody while playing it on the guitar. Once the melody is clearly fixed in your ear, use a neutral syllable as you vocalize — you'll find that this allows you more freedom to pursue your expressive ideas.

Those who are familiar with rehearsals and master classes know that conductors and fine instrumentalists are fluent in expressive vocalization. The quality of a musician's voice is of little importance — although conductors and instrumentalists rarely have fine voices, they strongly rely on vocalization to convey their expressive ideas.

Spare no effort to become fluent in vocalization — it's the most direct and effective means to becoming an expressive performer.[†]

[†]Expressive vocalization is an extension of pre-reading vocalization. For an explanation of vocalization in pre-reading, see *Learning the Classic Guitar, Part Two*, p. 13.

Applying Note-Grouping and Phrasing

Having acquired a basic understanding of note-grouping and phrasing, you're now ready to begin applying this knowledge in short melodies.

To play a melody expressively, you must become thoroughly familiar with the contrasts within the melody. You need to recognize contrasts in pitch and rhythm, then organize and convey them in a musically coherent way. Thus, as you approach each musical example, carry out the following steps:

1) Determine all figures and phrases.

2) Listen to the recording. Then, without the guitar, vocalize the example, applying note-grouping and phrasing through the use of rubato and dynamics.

3) Simultaneously vocalize and play the example on the guitar — vocalizing helps to guide your fingers toward more expressive playing.

∞ ∞ ∞ ∞ ∞ ∞ ∞

Your study of applied note-grouping and phrasing will begin with a simple melody. Ex. 31 contains both dialogue and continuous phrases (figures are marked with slurs; phrases are marked off with ∨):

Ex. 31

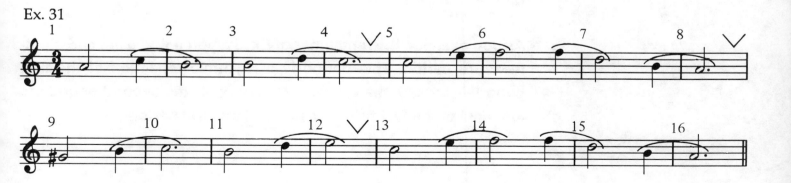

- Notice that the sequence of notes in the first two measures strongly indicates upbeat grouping — not only does attraction of the strong beat apply, but also attraction by duration and melodic attraction apply between the Do of the first measure and the Ti which follows.

- The half note of the first measure is a rhythmic syllable. The quarter note on the third beat is grouped with the dotted half note of the following measure. Thus, the first two-measure group contains a rhythmic syllable followed by a figure of two notes.

- Measures 3 and 4 repeat the rhythmic scheme of measures 1 and 2. They also melodically reflect the first two measures, but at a higher pitch. Thus, we've identified a four-measure dialogue phrase — measures 1 and 2 are the antecedent or statement, and measures 3 and 4 are the consequent or response.

- Now observe the next four measures. Although the change in direction and the downward skip between measures 6 and 7 seem to suggest a subtle separation and grouping, notice that the same rhythmic pattern recurs throughout the phrase, until it finally ends with the dotted half note in measure 8. Thus, these four measures are a continuous phrase.

- Notice that measures of $\left| \; \lozenge \quad \lozenge \; \right|$ provide a rhythmic similarity between the first two phrases (measures 1 through 4 and measures 5 through 8) — both phrases are also the same length. Our natural sense of order is so strong that we almost automatically feel the balance of the second phrase with the first. This balance of phrases produces a *period* in music.

- As you examine the remainder of Ex. 31, you'll find a second eight-measure period. This period is a rhythmic reflection of the first period — indeed, the last four measures of the second period are identical to the last four measures of the first period.

Applying Rubato and Dynamics

Your concern here is with two basic means of expression — rubato and dynamics. You'll begin by applying rubato and dynamics according to the degrees of melodic activity within Ex. 31. A rise in the melody signals an increase in activity which generally culminates at the high point. A fall in the melody signals a decrease in activity which normally subsides at the low point.

We express an increase in activity with a slight increase in tempo and a gentle rise in volume. We express a decrease in activity with a slackening of the tempo and a reduction of volume. To be most effective, you must smoothly execute these variations in volume and movement without giving the impression of an overall change in tempo. Try to imagine an ebb and flow of sound and movement which give a feeling of balance and proportion.

First you need to determine the pitch range of the melody. Then you need to observe the general shapes of figures and phrases, and also the pitch level on which they begin and end. With these aims in mind, reexamine Ex. 31:

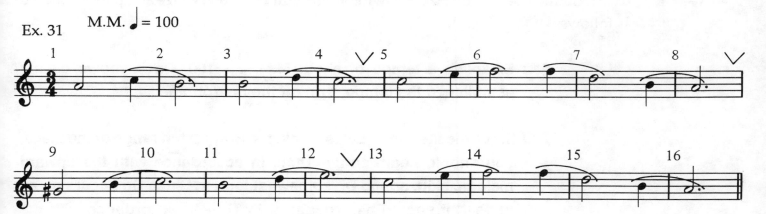

Ex. 31   M.M. ♩ = 100

- **Notice that the pitch range of the entire melody extends from Si (measure 9) to Fa (measures 6 and 14). The first antecedent (beginning in measure 1) begins with the tonic or keynote of the piece (La), makes a short skip upward, and ends by descending one scalewise step (measure 2). The consequent (measures 3 and 4) reflects the shape of the antecedent, but occupies a higher pitch range. Thus, the consequent is more active than the antecedent.**

- **The second phrase (measures 5 – 8), rising to the highest note (Fa) in this period, is very active for two measures (measures 5 and 6). Then the skip downward (to begin measure 7) and the descending melodic line (measures 7 and 8) indicate a sudden drop in activity which concludes on La — the pitch at which the piece began. Although the second period (measures 9–16) begins with the lowest note of the piece (Si), the first two figures, due to their upward endings (measures 9–10, and 11–12), imply more activity than was implied in earlier figures.**

- **Again, notice that the second phrase of the second period (measures 13 –16) is a repetition of the second phrase of the first period (measures 5 – 8). Also notice that, by ending on the tonic, a sense of rest is created — this is an example of melodic attraction. Thus, melodic attraction is often an important element in determining a phrase.**

This brief analysis gives you a framework of ideas for expressively performing Ex. 31. (Remember to vocalize first without the guitar, then vocalize and play.) Proceed as follows:

- ❏ **Establish a tempo of about M.M. ♩ = 100. Once you've clearly established the tempo, turn off the metronome.**

- ❏ **Since the first note (La) is within the lower pitch range of the piece, you should begin softly. Then, in accordance with the upward melodic skip, sound Do somewhat louder. Since Do occurs on an upbeat, it should be grouped with Ti — in accordance with the downward movement, Ti should be played somewhat softer than Do. This three-note group forms an antecedent.**

- ❏ **Since the consequent is on a higher pitch level, it's more active than the antecedent. You should play it in a manner similar to the antecedent, but with a slight increase in both volume and forward movement.**

- ❏ **Begin the second phrase *a tempo* (Italian, "at the original tempo," pronounced "ah *tem*-po"); the upward direction in the first two measures indicates an increase in activity which culminates with a**

Fa — the highest and most dramatic point in the first period. You should emphasize this *dramatic high point* with a *crescendo*, an expressive *ritard* (a gradual slowing of the tempo), and a slight accent.

❑ Since the first Fa has absorbed the main force of activity, the upbeat Fa should be played more softly — begin *a tempo,* and descend with a gradual decrease in volume and a slight *ritard* to end the first period.

❑ Melodically, the phrase in measures 9–12 differs markedly from the one in measures 1–4. The upward endings of both the antecedent and consequent are more active and thus call for a slightly stronger upbeat grouping. You can do this by increasing the delay of the upbeat — very slightly in the antecedent and a little more in the consequent. Also, be sure to conform dynamically to the melodic contour of the phrase — the antecedent in measures 9–10 should begin slightly louder than the first period (measures 1–8), and the consequent should begin louder still, with a slight *crescendo* to end the consequent more forcefully than the antecedent.

❑ The second phrase of the second period is identical to that of the first period, and so it should be played in a similar manner. The ending should be simple, direct, not too loud, and with a final *ritard* to conclude the melody.

Further Application of Upbeat Grouping

So far, you've applied upbeat grouping in Ex. 31 based on the attractions indicated in the music. As previously indicated, however, upbeat grouping is often highly effective even when it's not indicated in the music.

Ex. 32 is a more developed version of Ex. 31. Two quarter notes replace each half note, so that several measures now contain three consecutive quarter notes. This provides musical material with which you can practice applying both upbeat and downbeat grouping (see pp. 28–31).

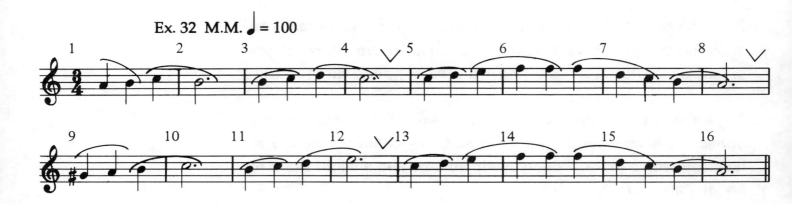

As you carry out the three-step procedure described on p. 35, observe the following:

- **With respect to phrases and periods, the general structure of Ex. 32 is the same as Ex. 31.**

- **Since the overall melodic contour of Ex. 32 is similar to Ex. 31, the dynamic considerations for Ex. 31 are also applicable to Ex. 32. Notice that the scalewise contour of Ex. 32 allows you to apply dynamics in a smoother, more gradual, and better proportioned manner.**

- **Downbeat grouping is effective in several measures containing three quarter notes. In measure 1, for example, La and Ti are a figure — they should be securely joined by *very slightly* rushing La towards Ti. This creates another level of subtle rhythmic activity within the measure.**

∾   ∾   ∾   ∾   ∾   ∾   ∾

Ex. 33 is a further development of Ex. 32, adding one note to the upbeat figures in measures 1–4, measures 7–8, and measures 9–12. This creates a more active and interesting three-note figure.

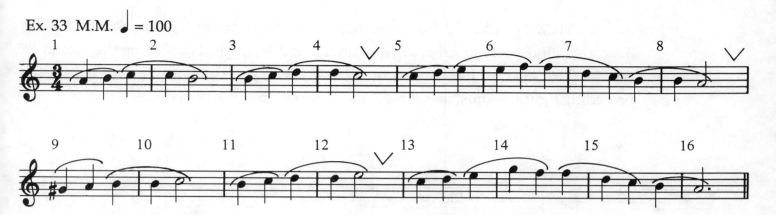

Ex. 33 M.M. ♩ = 100

Again, carry out the three-step procedure described on p. 35 — because of the added notes in Ex. 33, be sure to observe the following:

- **Play the beginning downbeat figure and the following upbeat in a manner similar to the way you played them in Ex. 32.**

- **Although there's no harmonic accompaniment to the melody, the note on the first beat of measures 2, 4, 6, and 8 *implies* a dissonance of considerable activity — thus, it should receive a slight accent and be held briefly before being gently resolved on the consonant and stable second beat.[†] (This also applies in measures 10, 12, and 14 of the second period.)**

- **Notice also that the upper range of the melody has been extended by one step to include So in measure 14. This So is the dramatic high point of the melody and should be approached with a *crescendo* and short *ritard*. Its resolution (Fa) should be somewhat quieter and held briefly before playing the upbeat Fa.**

[†]Students trained in music theory will recognize this as an implied *appoggiatura*.

NOTICE: The added dissonances in Ex. 33 create an interesting situation — you now have an optional way of grouping measures 6 and 14. Instead of playing the second Fa (on the third beat) of these measures as an upbeat, you could also group it with the preceding figure — thus, measures 7 and 15 would begin with a downbeat figure:

Ex. 34

This would be an effective contrast to the upbeat figures in the rest of the melody. Try it both ways and choose the one you find most appealing.

Creating Mood and Spirit

Now that you've progressed to the point of applying expression in a complete piece, you're ready to consider the overall meaning of a piece. Every piece — be it large or small — has its own mood and spirit. Thus, as you note the key and time signature of a piece, you should also note if the composer has supplied general indications of tempo, mood, and spirit.

Composers will often choose a title which suggests the intended character of the piece. Ex. 35, for example, is entitled "Folk Song" — this tells us that the piece should be performed in a lyrical manner.

Notice also that the composer has supplied an indication of the tempo. "Andante" is Italian for "walking" — thus, the piece should be played at a walking or moderate tempo, as confirmed by the metronome setting of ♩ = 88. "Andante" also suggests something about mood and spirit — it suggests that the piece should be played smoothly and quietly (as you would normally walk).

Creating a mood and spirit, however, goes far beyond what the composer can tell us. Your own experiences and emotions are a vital part of creating mood and spirit in music. A piece may suggest associations or experiences which are uniquely yours, conjuring images of a place you've visited, a person you know, a story you've heard, or an event in your life. Such imagery can be a powerful and creative resource for the expressive performer.

For example, "Folk Song" may suggest to you a sense of loss or bereavement. Or maybe you hear it as a gentle and melancholy reminder of an old friend or a loved one. Perhaps it suggests other folk songs in your memory. Any of these associations can be a catalyst for your expressive imagination. The experiences and emotions you bring to music will color and enrich the expression you choose to apply.[†]

You should add consideration of mood and spirit to the procedure given on p. 35. Thus, you should always carry out the following steps with any piece which you plan to perform:

1) Note the key and time signature, and also note if the composer has supplied general indications of tempo, mood, and spirit.

2) Determine all figures and phrases.

3) Without the guitar, vocalize the example, applying note-grouping and phrasing through the use of rubato and dynamics.

4) Simultaneously vocalize and play the example on the guitar.[††]

∞   ∞   ∞   ∞   ∞   ∞   ∞

Because of its added bass line, "Folk Song" can be effectively played at a somewhat slower tempo than the previous examples. To avoid confusion, you should for now think of the bass as having no distinct function of its own in grouping. Rather, a bass note immediately following a melody note should be grouped with that note. The repeated basses generally should be played in strict rhythm, with a slight ritard at phrase endings and a more pronounced ritard to end the piece. Since the bass functions solely as accompaniment, it should be played more *piano* (softly) than the melody.

[†]*To the teacher:* Since "Folk Song" is a rather modest piece, some may think it's stretching interpretive credibility to imply that this piece has much expressive potential. But beginning to play expressively is a challenge, and approaching more complex music at this point would pose unnecessary difficulties for most students.
[††]If the meaning of "vocalize" is unclear, review "Approaching Expression through Vocalization," p. 34.

Folk Song

Ex. 35 Andante (M.M. ♩ = 88)

A.S.

"Folk Dance" (Ex. 36) is a rhythmic variation of "Folk Song." (This is Solo No. 8 R.V. from *Learning the Classic Guitar, Part Two*, p. 50.)

As you did with "Folk Song," you should consider the mood and spirit of the piece you're about to play. Cultivate this approach as a habit, making it a consistent consideration in all the music you play.

Notice that the rhythmic contrasts written into "Folk Dance" are more active than the more uniform note values of "Folk Song." Indeed, the title "Folk Dance" indicates that the composer intends the piece to be dance-like. Thus, in contrast to "Folk Song," you should approach "Folk Dance" with more energy, and clearer, more pronounced rhythms.

Before playing "Folk Dance," you should consider the melody separately from the basses:

• **"Folk Song" and "Folk Dance" contain the same successive pitches, have the same range and rise and fall of the melody, and the same number of notes in the antecedent and consequent of the first and third phrases. The main differences are the dotted-quarter/eighth-note rhythms, and measures 5–8 and 13–16, which now contain dialogue instead of continuous phrases.**

• **The distinctive rhythmic pattern of "Folk Dance" centers on the dotted quarter note followed by an eighth. The eighth note should be grouped with its following quarter note or dotted quarter note.**

• **Notice that, except in measures 6 and 14, the eighth note in the melody precedes the third beat. This gives strength and momentum to the normally weak third beat as it yields to the powerful attraction of the metric pulse.**

• **In measures 6 and 14, the eighth note on the last half of the third beat is strongly attracted to and emphasizes the metric pulse.**

You should begin by vocalizing "Folk Dance," aiming for a tempo of about M.M. ♩ = 88. Although your overall approach should be similar to that of "Folk Song," the rhythmic changes in "Folk Dance" require special consideration. Proceed as follows:

❏ **After beginning quietly with the dotted quarter note, connect the first eighth note to the third beat, and connect the third beat firmly to the metric pulse of the following measure. Resolve more quietly on the second beat to end the antecedent.**

❏ **Increase the momentum as the consequent continues to ascend — begin at about the same volume as the Ti in measure 2, and then slightly delay the eighth note, leaning it more forcefully on the third beat. This builds activity which then culminates on the first beat of the following measure. (This ends the first phrase.)**

❏ **Begin the second phrase (measures 5–8) at about the same volume as the Do which ends the first phrase. Quickly *crescendo* to culminate on Mi (measure 6), and slightly *ritard* to resolve on Fa.**

❏ **Resume *a tempo,* connecting the Fa ending measure 6 to the following Re (forming a two-note figure), and slacken the pace slightly to end the first period.**

❏ **Begin the second period (measures 9–16) softly. Since the antecedent ends by ascending, its greater activity should be reflected dynamically with a slight *crescendo.***

❏ **Begin the consequent (measure 11) somewhat more *piano* than the Do in measure 10, and apply a little more energy, ending a bit more *forte* (loudly) than the antecedent.**

❏ **Begin the last phrase (measure 13) *mezzo forte* (mf, moderately loud), *crescendo* to *forte* and with a slight *ritard* on So, and then quietly resolve on Fa. Resume *a tempo* for the next figure (the eighth note Fa and dotted quarter note Re), and then *diminuendo* (gradually decrease in volume) and *ritard* to end the piece.**

Folk Dance

Ex. 36

A.S.

Note-Grouping in Quadruple Meter

"Andante I" (Ex. 37) introduces the application of note-grouping in quadruple meter. Unlike triple meter (which has a strong beat followed by two weak beats), quadruple meter has alternating strong and weak beats. Although the two meters differ markedly in rhythmic feeling, your approach to applying expression should be similar for both.

Although the range of the melody is rather narrow — from Ti on the third line of the staff to So on the first space above the staff — you should still respond dynamically to each rise and fall of the melody.

∾   ∾   ∾   ∾   ∾   ∾   ∾

Since you're focusing on learning to apply expression through upbeat grouping and phrasing, you'll begin your analysis of "Andante I" by determining all upbeat figures and phrases (consider the melody separately from the bass):

- **As previously explained, the strong beats in quadruple meter are 1 and 3; the weak beats are 2 and 4. Thus, upbeat grouping will be 2, 3 and 4, 1.**

- **When the first beat of a measure isn't preceded by an upbeat (for example, measures 1 and 3), the first beat is a syllable and should be phrased with the following upbeat figure.**

- **Notice that the half note in the measure 2 clearly defines the end of an antecedent. A glance at measures 3 and 4 confirms that they're the consequent. This completes the first dialogue phrase.**

- **Since there's no rhythmic separation in the next four measures, they constitute a continuous phrase. Notice that this phrase seems to balance with the first phrase — thus, it completes the first period.**

- **The next eight measures (9–16) rhythmically reflect the first eight measures. Since this provides an effective balance with the first period, you might expect the piece to end here. But music doesn't always consist of perfectly balanced groups — variety and surprise often greatly add musical appeal.**

• "Andante I" has a four-measure extension (measures 17–20) which begins in the same manner as the previous four measures. These four measures can be regarded as either a reemphasis or an echo of the preceding phrase. A reemphasis would require more energy and movement — an echo would require less. Choose one or the other, and try to make your choice clear in your playing. Whichever approach you choose, you should end with a ritard to convey a feeling of finality.

Andante I

A. S.

Summary

In expressively playing the previous examples, you've made the same kind of judgments and decisions required to interpret even the most challenging concert pieces. You've considered the relationships of notes, figures, phrases, and periods. Further, you've made entirely personal decisions about how to perform each piece expressively. Whatever your level of accomplishment, from beginner to concert artist, you alone must make such decisions.

Although anyone can acquire a general impression of what to do and why it should be done, expression becomes an elusive subject when you begin to consider how to carry it out. The meaning of terms such as "softly," "loudly," "subtle," "forward movement," and "slackening of pace" are indefinite and constantly variable — yet they are also crucial. Thus, your effectiveness as an expressive musician depends entirely on how you perceive and apply these terms.

Ultimately, expression is the intuitive application of the concepts you've learned through careful study and practice. Without your intuitive sense of aesthetic proportion and effect, these concepts of expression are of little value. Thus, expression is true artistic creativity — the harmonious blending of knowledge and intuition.

Pieces for Study

The seven pieces which follow are short studies by four 19th century guitarists/composers. I've chosen these pieces for their musical diversity and for their value as studies in note-grouping and phrasing. Prepare each piece carefully, listen to it on the recording, and then practice playing it as expressively as you can.

∞   ∞   ∞   ∞   ∞   ∞   ∞

The first two pieces are by one of the greatest Spanish musicians of his time, Fernando Sor (1778–1839).[†] Opus 60 was his last work for solo guitar, which he entitled "Introduction to the Study of the Guitar."

The first of these pieces, Op. 60, No. 13, was published without a tempo indication. Its flowing character, however, seems to suggest a walking tempo (indicated here as "Andante"). Since this piece consists mainly of eighth values, the metronome setting is quite slow.

[†]An excellent biographical treatise is Brian Jeffery's *Fernando Sor, Composer and Guitarist*. The same author has also edited a nine-volume set of Sor's complete works for the guitar. All are published by Tecla Editions, Preachers' Court, Charterhouse, London ECIM 6AS, England.

Op. 60, No. 13

F. Sor

Andante M.M. ♩ = 60

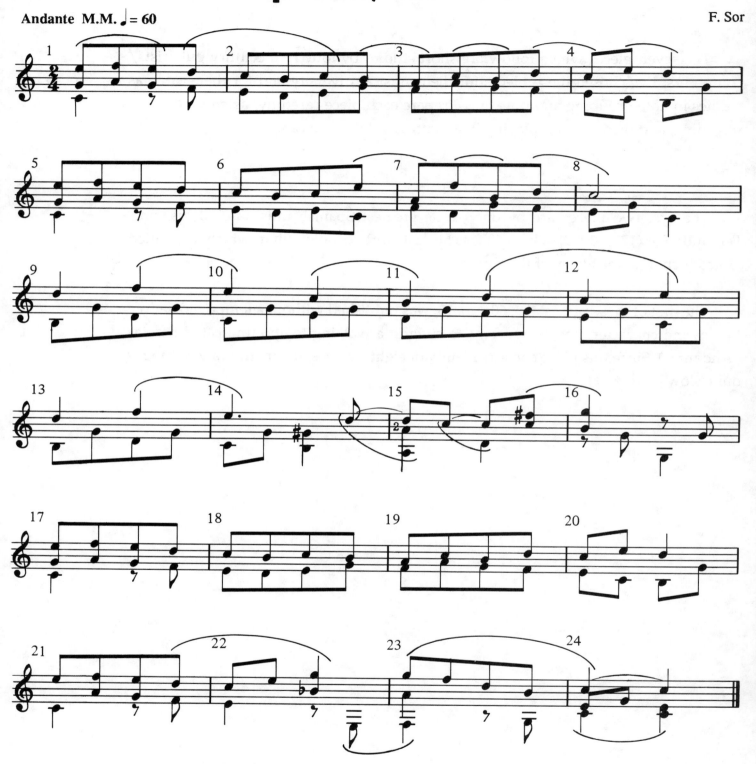

The second piece, Op. 60, No. 14, was published with the tempo indication "Andante." The considerable difference in metronome settings between this and the previous Andante is due to differences in rhythmic structure — while the previous piece consists mainly of eighth values, this piece consists mostly of quarter values.

Andante: Op. 60, No. 14

F. Sor

The following piece is from the guitar method by Spanish guitarist Dionisio Aguado (1784–1849). Aguado often performed duets with his friend Fernando Sor. This short piece, entitled simply "Lesson No. 15," was published without a tempo indication. Its distinctive dance-like character, however, indicates that it should be played brightly.

Lesson No. 15

D. Aguado

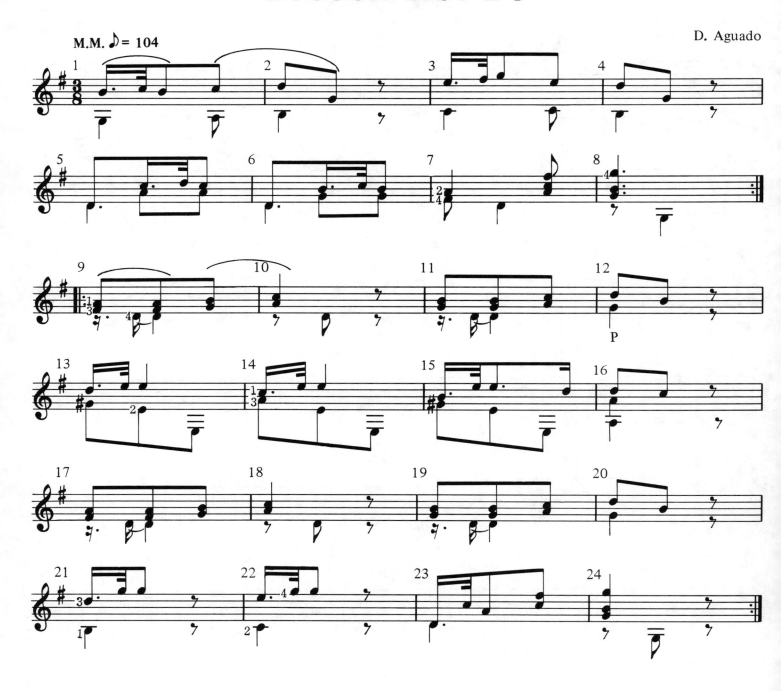

The next piece is by the Italian guitar virtuoso and composer, Mauro Giuliani (1781–1829).[†] It can be found in Volume 14 of *The Complete Works of Mauro Giuliani*, edited by Brian Jeffery and published by Tecla Editions.

Andante: Op. 139, No. 1

M. Giuliani

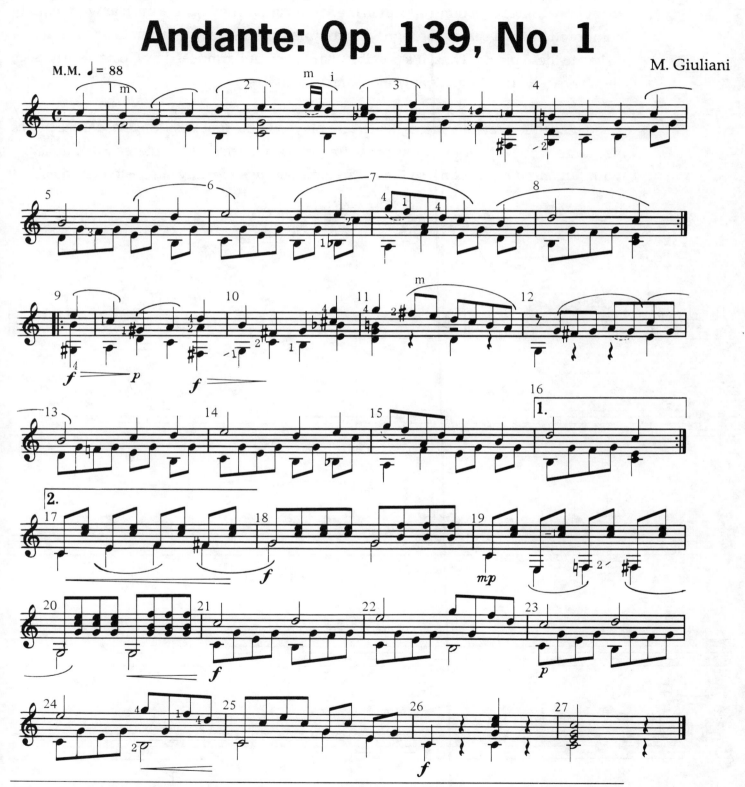

[†]Thomas F. Heck has written a comprehensive treatise on the life of Giuliani. Presented as a doctoral thesis at Yale University in 1970, this invaluable work is entitled *The Birth of the Classical Guitar and its Cultivation in Vienna, Reflected in the Career and Compositions of Mauro Giuliani (d. 1829)*. It's available in book form from University Microfilms, Ann Arbor, MI.

The last three pieces appear in the revision of Sor's guitar method by the French guitarist/composer, Napoleon Coste (1806–1883). Each of these pieces is identified simply as a "Lesson" along with the appropriate number in the order of its appearance in the book. Since they don't appear in the Sor's original method, it's unclear who actually composed them. A search through Sor's complete works (see the footnote on p. 51) failed to locate these pieces. Thus, it's possible that they were composed by Coste. In any case, they're excellent note-grouping and phrasing studies.

Unlike the previous pieces, which are played in the first position, these three pieces use notes in the higher positions of the fingerboard. Each of these pieces was published without tempo indications, so the metronome settings are only suggested tempos.

Lesson No. 9

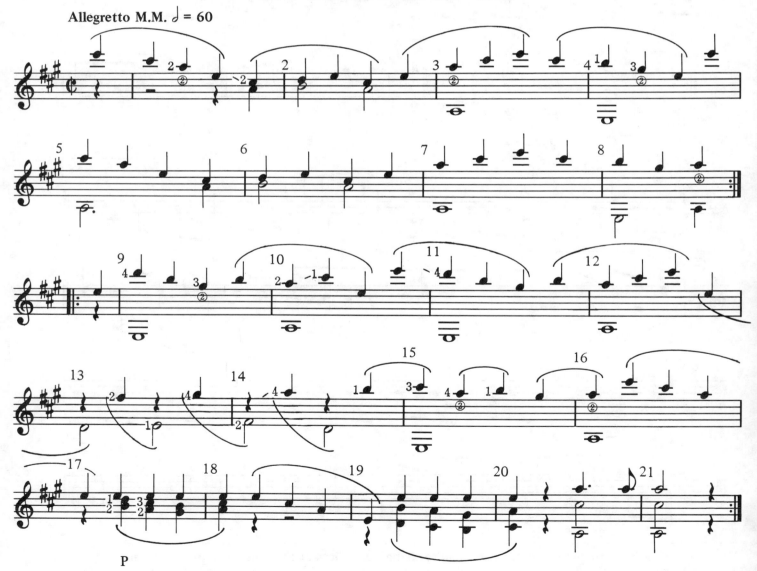

Lesson No. 12

Lesson No. 13

Performance Development

Introduction

The Cause of Performance Anxiety

The problems of playing for an audience are well known. Most students and even many concert musicians approach performance with anxiety — sometimes severe anxiety. Thus, although sharing music with others should be a uniquely gratifying and enjoyable experience, regrettably it often is not.

This situation is entirely unnecessary. Performance anxiety isn't an inevitable consequence of playing for others — rather, it's the result of improper training.

> **Students experience anxiety during performance because they attempt to perform without adequate preparation. Thus, they build habits of insecurity into their approach to performing. Indeed, even many concert performers developed habits of performance anxiety when they were young — habits which, throughout their lives, they never find a way to overcome.**

Most students attempt to perform pieces without having achieved the ability to play them confidently — without mistakes or hesitations — during practice. Encouraged by their teacher and friends, or through their own drive to perform, these students hope that somehow they'll be able to do in performance what they can't securely do in practice. Further, they're not taught that performing with confidence is an acquired skill. Thus, they're never provided the necessary information and opportunities for learning this skill.

Here then is the true cause of the performance anxiety which is rampant among students and even concert musicians. Once habits of anxiety are established, they can be replaced only through a great deal of patient and well-directed study.

Evaluating Your Situation

In performance, continuity and confidence are essential — you must be confident that you can play a piece from beginning to end without hesitations. To acquire secure habits of continuity and confidence, you must carefully apply Aim-Directed Movement (ADM) at all times during both practice and performance.

The essence of ADM is seeing ahead as you play. The notes behind you are no longer important — you should concentrate only on the notes which lie ahead. Only by learning to focus and sustain your concentration through ADM will you be able to perform music confidently without hesitations.

Always remember that acquiring the ability to focus and sustain your concentration begins in the practice room, and that confusion and error are fatal to concentration. Thus, you must learn to recognize and avoid confusion and error during study and practice. The following are common examples of confusion and error:

- **MAKING FALSE STARTS: During their practice sessions, misdirected students often make one or more false starts before finally beginning to play the piece. Indeed, they may even make false starts within the piece itself. Without having developed the confidence that they can play the piece from beginning to end without hesitations, these students inevitably build habits of insecurity into their ability to perform.**

  Bear in mind that you don't have the option of making false starts during a performance — once you begin playing, you must play to the end of the piece without stopping. Thus, since you don't want to make false starts during a performance, you should avoid false starts during practice.

- **THE "DOUBLE-ERROR REFLEX": When students miss a note, they tend to dart back and try to correct their mistake. Thus, they make two errors:**
  1) They miss the note.
  2) In attempting to correct their mistake, they break the continuity of the music. This tendency is often so deeply ingrained that it's virtually a reflex — what I call the "double-error reflex."

  The double-error reflex indicates that you've practiced without concentrating on seeing ahead as you play. Thus, you haven't built the habits of concentration essential for performing with continuity and confidence.

You can avoid the double-error reflex by constantly emphasizing ADM in your practice sessions. By constantly applying ADM, you'll gradually acquire the habit of always seeing ahead as you play.

• "GRABBING" FOR NOTES: When misdirected students encounter a passage that's not clear in their minds, they often "go for it" anyway and hope for the best. This is a very dangerous habit. Even if these students happen to play the correct notes, they almost certainly experience insecurity.

If you're grabbing for notes in this manner, you're acquiring neither the habit of ADM nor the concentration that ADM demands. Instead, you're acquiring habits of confusion and error.

∾   ∾   ∾   ∾   ∾   ∾   ∾

You can acquire secure habits of concentration only by being very sensitive to confusion during your study and practice. Thus, you should learn to anticipate confusion before it causes you to make errors. By recognizing and systematically eliminating confusion, you'll gradually develop habits of continuity and confidence.

Regarding Technique and Memorization

The purpose of performance development isn't to improve your technique or memorization. If you've acquired habits of insecurity in either technique or your ability to memorize music, you must recognize them as serious impediments to your development as a secure performer. Thus, you need to carefully and honestly evaluate all areas of your ability to play the guitar.

You'll find information for correcting technical deficiencies in *Learning the Classic Guitar, Part One* — in particular, be sure you thoroughly understand the section entitled "Approaching Guitar Study" (pp. 1–8). Also, you should be fluent with the four-step memorization procedure in *Learning the Classic Guitar, Part Two* (see "Memorizing Music," pp. 212–220).

Approaching Performance Development

Performance refers to playing the guitar in a situation which causes you concern. The *size* of your audience isn't the issue — playing for only one person may cause you extreme concern. Indeed, making a recording can be a vivid performance experience, even though there's no audience present. Thus, *your feeling of concern* is the criterion for defining a performance.

Naturally this concern excites you. Your excitement can be pleasant and beneficial, enabling you to play more expressively when performing than when practicing alone. Or your excitement can be unpleasant and harmful, adversely affecting all aspects of your playing. Whether you experience positive or negative excitement is directly influenced by your attitudes and emotions toward performing.

Although becoming a secure player in the privacy of your practice room is an essential prerequisite for performance development, it's not a meaningful criterion of your ability as a guitarist. Sharing with others is your prime motivation for playing the guitar — only when you can successfully perform for others will your sense of accomplishment be fully realized.

> Thus, in evaluating your ability as a guitarist, how well you play while alone in your practice room is irrelevant. Performance is the only meaningful criterion of your playing.

Performance Anxiety and Negative Concerns

Uneasiness, nervousness, and nausea are common in even mild instances of anxiety. More severe problems — confusion and loss of concentration and control — lead to inaccuracy and memory lapses. These problems leave a performer feeling embarrassed and discouraged. Indeed, severe performance anxiety is so impressive and enduring that it often continues to impede a player's performance ability long after he or she has acquired a high level of technical and musical proficiency. Uncorrected, anxiety can also cause serious problems of muscle function which may eventually lead to injury.[†]

In the early stages of your performance development, some anxiety is virtually inevitable. But you can begin to eliminate it once you understand its causes. Anxiety is caused by three negative concerns:

1) CONCERN ABOUT BEING THE CENTER OF ATTENTION. This is deeply rooted in the human psyche. Uneasiness at being the center of attention begins at an early age — most children will look away and withdraw if they sense that they're being watched by strangers. In such a situation, even adults may react with uneasiness, embarrassment, or outright antagonism.

2) CONCERN ABOUT YOUR PLAYING ABILITY. We all have a natural fear of failing in the presence of others. Indeed, most students are plagued with self-doubt when approaching a performance: Will I be able to play the difficult passages well? Will I have a major memory lapse? Will I appear awkward and inept?

These first two concerns are a normal part of being human — everyone experiences them to some degree. But the third concern is an inevitable consequence of your study and practice. Although not immediately obvious, it's perhaps the most important negative concern of all:

3) CONCERN ABOUT ERRORS. Learning to play even simple pieces on the guitar demands a very specific focus of concentration — you must develop an acute sensitivity to imminent errors as well as to technical and musical problems. Thus, by the time you've acquired the skill to play even relatively simple pieces, you've established strong habits of concern about errors.

Your habit of concern about errors is essential for *learning* to play the guitar — it enables you to recognize your deficiencies so you can work to correct them. So why is it a negative concern during performance development? There are two reasons:

1) During a performance, stopping to correct an error disrupts the continuity of your playing. Once an error occurs, you can't undo it. Thus, being sensitive to errors during performance serves no purpose.

[†]See "Repetitive Strain Injury," *Part One*, p. 124.

2) If you're sensitive to errors as you perform, an error will inevitably distract you. As a student, however, it would be unrealistic for you to expect to give an errorless performance. Indeed, even the most accomplished players occasionally make minor errors during a performance. Thus, being concerned about errors is actually harmful when you're performing — *in fact, it virtually guarantees that you'll make errors.*

Being sensitive to errors is a distraction which hinders your ability to concentrate. Thus, you must learn to redirect your concentration away from errors. When performing, you should concentrate only on playing the music — using solfege, counting, and Aim-Directed Movement (ADM) to maintain your concentration. You can more effectively maintain your concentration if you have a clearly defined procedure for dealing with errors during a performance.

Dealing with Errors During Performance

There are two kinds of errors which may occur during a performance:

• *Minor error:* **This is any error which doesn't cause you to become confused or to hesitate. As long as you can continue playing without confusion, you should disregard minor errors whenever they occur.**

• *Major error:* **This is any error which forces you to hesitate. If a major error occurs, you should strive to remain in complete control. Don't focus on the error itself — instead, concentrate on dealing with it in the most graceful and effective manner.**

In order of preference, you should deal with a major error in one of the following ways:

1) Play the next note and continue on.
2) Skip to the next figure or phrase which is clear in your mind.
3) Skip back to the beginning of the entire passage or section and execute it on the second try.
4) Start over from the beginning of the piece.
5) As a last resort, proceed to the next piece in your program. (If there's no other piece in your program, terminate your performance with a courteous bow and exit.)

Once you've dealt with a major error through one of these five ways, you should concentrate exclusively on playing the music. Don't dwell on a major error through the rest of your performance — to do so would virtually guarantee that you'll make another error.

∾   ∾   ∾   ∾   ∾   ∾   ∾

Learning to deal positively with errors during performance will be challenging at first. No conscientious player wants to make errors — the composer didn't write errors, and major errors can be distracting to the audience. Further, you've practiced very hard to avoid making errors. Thus, even a few minor errors during a performance can be extremely discouraging.

But you must learn to avoid this discouragement. An occasional error is inevitable — although we should always strive for perfection as we practice, being human, we can never actually achieve it. Thus, you need to cultivate an entirely nonjudgmental attitude toward your playing as you perform. Once you begin a performance, you should concentrate only on playing as well as you can — *perform for the sake of sharing music on whatever level you can.*

Replacing Negative Concerns with Positive Concerns

Most students receive little or no meaningful training in dealing with negative concerns. Usually they're told that if they perform often enough their anxiety will gradually disappear. For many students, however, this is untrue. Indeed, the more they try to overcome their negative concerns, the more anxious they become. Without proper training, their anxiety will continue to grow until it hinders all aspects of their playing.

You can't diminish anxiety by dwelling on negative concerns. Instead, you must learn to concentrate on positive concerns:

• **CULTIVATE A POSITIVE ATTITUDE TOWARD YOUR LISTENERS. You need your listeners. Whether you're performing for a large audience or a modest gathering of friends, they're the reason for your study and practice. Further, your listeners need you. Many regard the ability to play classical music as an exceptional accomplishment, implying refinement, sensitivity, and taste. These are appealing quali-**

ties, and they're perhaps the main reason why many people are attracted to the classic guitar. Thus, you should regard your listeners with affection and appreciation. They'll sense and appreciate this attitude.

You can cultivate a positive attitude only through sustained effort. The benefits, however, are well worth the effort. Since you inevitably carry your daily attitudes into performing, nurturing a positive and friendly attitude toward others not only makes your daily life more pleasant, it also makes learning to perform easier and more rewarding.

- NEVER IMPOSE YOUR CONCERNS AND EXPECTATIONS ON YOUR LISTEN-ERS. Misdirected players often berate their own performances. Since errors disturb them, they assume that errors are equally disturbing to the audience. Some players feel compelled to apologize for their playing when a listener tries to compliment them. This behavior is not only unprofessional, it's also rude — it implies that the listener is too stupid to recognize a bad performance.

This behavior stems from a misunderstanding of what listeners actually hear. *Most people don't notice minor errors, and they're not terribly concerned about the errors they do hear.* Even professional musicians prefer to listen to the overall effect of a piece rather than individual passages. Bear in mind that your listeners aren't aware of how you intend to play. Their impression is always general rather than specific. Most listeners simply want to enjoy your playing. Allow them that pleasure.

Summary

To perform well, you must have confidence in your ability to perform. The most effective way to gain this confidence is by building on positive performance experiences. Thus, performance development is designed to create an environment which assures success. By gradually building your confidence in successively more realistic performances, you'll eventually be able to perform confidently in any situation.

The keys to performance development are as follows:

- **CONTINUITY AND CONFIDENCE: To perform with continuity and confidence, you must acquire the ability to see ahead as you play. Thus, you must constantly apply ADM during both practice and performance development — this is the most efficient way to acquire secure habits of concentration.**

- **YOUR ATTITUDE TOWARD ERRORS: Whether you're performing for one person or a thousand, you should maintain a completely non-judgmental attitude toward errors. Develop two entirely separate attitudes — one for study and practice, the other for performing. When learning to play and memorize a piece, always strive for perfection. By eliminating confusion and error in your practice room, you're improving your ability to perform securely and confidently. *But never be disturbed by errors during a performance — instead, concentrate on playing as well as you can.***

- **YOUR ATTITUDE TOWARD YOUR LISTENERS:**
  1. Perform for the sake of sharing on whatever level you can.
  2. Cultivate a positive attitude toward your listeners.
  3. Never impose your concerns and expectations on your listeners.

∞   ∞   ∞   ∞   ∞   ∞   ∞

Don't expect to acquire these skills and attitudes overnight. Developing habits of continuity and confidence through ADM is a gradual process. Further, negative performance concerns can be deeply rooted, particularly if you've experienced severe anxiety during past peformances. But over and over again, students with performance backgrounds of embarassment and failure have learned to become secure and confident performers. With proper study and practice, you too can develop the ability to perform.

Beginning Performance Development

Before You Begin

Confidence grows from success. Thus, you need to establish conditions which will ensure success from the beginning of your performance development. You must begin with the selection and preparation of a piece for performance. Students often try to perform without sufficient preparation — either they can't securely execute the piece, or they haven't memorized it clearly enough.

In performance, every problem of technique or memorization is magnified — if you can't securely play a piece without mistakes or hesitations during practice, you won't be able to perform it securely. Thus, as you begin performance development, choose relatively short and simple pieces which you can securely play from memory at an effective tempo.

The Practice Performance

The degree of your familiarity with performance will influence the level of your performance excitement. To concentrate securely on playing, you need to become familiar with the performance situation. The practice performance is a situation in which you play a piece while imagining that an audience is present.

Proceed as follows:

❑ **You'll begin by practicing performance in the privacy of your study room. Turn your chair in a direction opposite from usual and imagine that an audience is present.**

❑ **Perform the piece in its entirety and without hesitations to your imaginary audience. Solfege aloud as you play. Concentrate on ADM — visualizing your finger movements on the guitar — and disregard any minor errors.**

❑ *Above all, don't stop!* Continue playing to the end of the piece. If you can't play the entire piece without hesitations, you haven't memorized the piece securely enough.

❑ When you can confidently play in the preceding situation, practice performing in places other than your practice room. To amplify your sound, try closely facing a corner, and imagine you're onstage facing an attentive audience. With practice, your imaginary audience will become increasingly vivid.

∞   ∞   ∞   ∞   ∞   ∞   ∞

The importance of practice performances can't be overemphasized. Thus, you should devote a substantial portion of your daily practice to this procedure. Recording your practice performance is also very helpful, especially if you listen to the recording when the performance is still fresh in your mind.

Establishing Your Concentration

Seated before an audience, in the final moment before you begin playing, you must direct your concentration away from the audience. To do this most securely, you need something specific on which to concentrate. Thus, you'll find the following procedure to be extremely beneficial:

❑ Check the tuning of your guitar.

❑ Breathe deeply several times.

❑ Silently solfege and visualize the first well-defined phrase of the piece you're about to play.

❑ Just before beginning to play, clearly set the tempo in your mind by silently counting.

You should establish this routine from the beginning of your performance development. In an actual performance situation, carrying out a consistent routine before beginning to play yields the following benefits:

- **It directs your attention away from the audience.**
- **It gives you time to gain composure.**
- **It creates an atmosphere of expectancy in the audience.**

Always follow this routine, regardless of how formal or informal the performance. As you become a more secure performer, this routine will become a habit, and you'll be able to carry it out quite rapidly. Eventually you'll be able to establish your concentration at will in any performance situation.

The Two Kinds of Performances

You'll continue your progressive approach to performance with two kinds of practice performances:

- *Developmental Performance (DP):* In a DP, you gradually learn to control your performance excitement in the presence of an audience. You intentionally approach the tempo and rhythms with flexibility, playing slowly, even pausing if necessary to refocus your concentration. Your aim isn't necessarily to play expressively — rather, your aim is to direct your concentration away from the audience, concentrating instead on playing the music. You'll still be sufficiently aware of the audience to be excited, but your excitement should be consistently positive. A DP allows you the time and freedom to grow accustomed to performing without the fear of failure.

- *Expressive Performance (EP):* This is the last step before an actual performance. Your aim is to interpret the music in the most appealing manner. Since pauses or hesitations are distractions, they aren't intentionally allowed in an EP. On a high level, an EP is a matter of spirit, spontaneity, and mutual expectancy between you and the audience. It creates an emotionally charged atmosphere, inspiring a level of expression beyond what you could achieve in your practice room.

The main difference between your approach to a DP and an EP is your intent. In a DP, your intent is to develop the ability to concentrate on the things which lead to positive performance excitement. In an EP, your intent is to apply this positive excitement in an actual performance situation.

Developmental Performance Procedure

When you've satisfactorily completed several practice performances, invite a friend or family member to be your audience. Explain the purpose of a DP, then proceed in the following manner:

❏ Sit with the guitar in approximate playing position. Now take time to position the guitar properly. Carefully and quietly check the tuning. These steps will help establish your concentration.

❏ Breathe deeply several times — this helps control your excitement.

❏ Silently solfege and visualize the first well-defined phrase. *Take as much time as you need!* Don't begin playing until your concentration is clear and focused.

❏ Clearly set the tempo in your mind by counting, then begin playing.

❏ Perform the piece from beginning to end, silently counting or solfeging as you play. *Don't rush the tempo* — play as slowly as necessary to sustain your concentration.

❏ If your concentration begins to lapse as you're playing, deliberately pause. *Maintain self-control!* Regain your concentration and visualize the next passage accurately and clearly. Solfege aloud if necessary. Then continue with the note following the last note you played. If you can't recall and visualize the passage after a short pause, skip to the next passage which you can clearly remember.

❏ When you play, tilt your head slightly forward and toward your left knee. From this position, you can turn your head slightly to the right or the left to glance at either hand, and by looking slightly downward you'll avoid eye contact with your listener.

❏ **While playing, maintain a pleasant yet serious facial expression, neither smiling nor appearing overly stern. Avoid grimacing, excessive nodding, loud breathing, or any other mannerism that would distract your listener.**

∞   ∞   ∞   ∞   ∞   ∞   ∞

It's extremely important to maintain self-control and finish playing the piece. In a DP, a deliberate pause to regain self-control should not be considered an error. An error is a missed note, an unintentionally displaced rhythm, or an incorrect fingering — anything caused by confusion and lack of control. If you miss a note, avoid the common tendency to go back and grab for the missed note before continuing. This tendency stems from faulty practice habits.

Above all, control yourself! Never appear frustrated, embarrassed, disgusted, or unpleasant in any way. Listeners quickly sense such behavior and become uneasy. Always maintain a confident and professional appearance.

You could learn much about performing from the great Polish pianist, Jan Ignace Paderewski. Years ago, during a Carnegie Hall recital, Paderewski experienced a major memory lapse. He repeated a phrase 13 times before finally continuing the piece. Paderewski actually appeared to enjoy the episode, and he received a rousing ovation. Clearly, listeners will forgive rather serious flaws as long as you appear pleasant and keep playing.

If you suffer from severe anxiety, you may need to pause frequently to regain your concentration. *But once you begin the piece, always play through to the end.* If you falter and simply can't continue, conscientiously evaluate your situation. Your problem was very likely due to one or more of the following reasons:

1) YOU'VE SELECTED A PIECE THAT'S TOO DIFFICULT: The purpose of performance development is to learn to deal positively with the excitement of playing for an audience. You should have no technical problems in playing the piece.

2) YOU'RE TRYING TO PLAY AT A TEMPO THAT'S TOO FAST: This is a very common mistake. Remember, your aim is to acquire secure habits of sustained concentration during a performance situation. Thus, you should maintain a tempo at which you can clearly visualize your finger movements on the guitar.

3) YOU HAVEN'T SECURELY MEMORIZED THE PIECE: Remember, if you neglect any step in the memorization procedure, the entire process will be flawed. These flaws are amplified when you try to perform.

4) YOU'RE DWELLING ON NEGATIVE PERFORMANCE CONCERNS: If severe performance anxiety forced you to a halt, you've had a powerful demonstration of how debilitating negative concerns can be. Review pp. 66–67, then intensify your efforts to consistently concentrate on positive performance concerns.

∞ ∞ ∞ ∞ ∞ ∞ ∞

Remember, there's no such thing as failure during a DP. The DP is a learning situation, and you can learn from every performance. Even if you had to stop in the middle of a DP, you've now acquired a vivid experience of an actual performance situation — use this experience in your daily practice sessions. Above all, be persistent. If one performance is unsatisfactory, evaluate your problem and decide on a solution. Then try again.

Perform frequently and as many times as necessary to gain confidence in your ability to concentrate while playing for someone. When you feel secure performing for one person, invite two or three more people to be your audience.

Be keenly aware of your reactions before, during, and after performing. Are your thoughts positive or negative? Are you happy and appreciative for the opportunity to share with others, or are you dwelling on feelings of inadequacy? Habits of attitude form quickly — thus, it's essential to maintain a positive attitude toward performance. Evaluate and accept your development realistically, and fix your thoughts on what you can do, not what you can't do. Just as you've developed the ability to play the guitar, you can develop the ability to perform with confidence.

Approaching the Formal DP

When you've acquired the ability to perform confidently for two or three people, you're ready to carry out a formal DP. A formal DP involves an audience of students who share an interest in performance development. Ideally, you would enroll as a special student in a performance development class offered by a local college guitar program. If this is impossible, however, find a group of mutually interested people — perhaps in connection with a guitar society. This group could include musicians other than guitarists. Your group may be small, but if the DP is carried out formally it will be effective.

A formal DP simulates an actual recital, except that DP procedures are applied. Again, you intentionally approach tempo and rhythms with flexibility, playing slowly, even pausing if necessary. A formal DP, however, now includes the customary exchange between the audience and performer. This exchange is so well established that most of us probably have never considered its importance:

- **The performer appears before the audience and walks directly to the chair.**

- **The audience applauds; this applause is a greeting to the performer.**

- **The performer responds by bowing; this conveys, "Thank you for the warm reception. I'm glad to be here."**

- **The performer sits and proceeds to play.**

- **The performer indicates either the end of the piece or an extended break in the program.**

- **The audience responds by applauding, as either a show of courtesy or appreciation.**

- **The performer stands and bows, again to indicate appreciation for the audience's applause.**

Thus, there's an exchange of courtesies from the moment the performer appears until the end of the performance. The warmth with which a performer is received is strongly influenced by the performer's appearance and conduct — sometimes termed "stage presence."

Learning Effective Stage Conduct

Good stage conduct is essential for any aspiring performer. You must be confident that the audience will react favorably to your appearance and conduct. This confidence will increase your ability to perform well. Even mediocre musicians can receive a warm response if they exhibit exceptionally appealing stage conduct.

The importance of effective stage conduct is often overlooked in the training of student performers. Indeed, effective stage conduct appears so natural and easy that it often goes unnoticed — except perhaps for our admiration of its gracefulness. Only when stage conduct is badly carried out does the audience sense that something's wrong.

For most student performers, effective stage conduct is neither natural nor easy. Thus, effective stage conduct is an acquired skill which — like every other area of musical study — requires a great deal of well-directed practice.

Effective stage conduct serves two immediate purposes: It creates a receptive atmosphere of expectancy and enthusiasm in the audience, and it gives you a feeling of confidence. Further, as a student learning to perform, you'll find that focusing on stage conduct will direct your attention toward the act of performing and away from the audience.

To develop an appealing stage conduct, you should cultivate the following qualities:

- **Appear graceful, yet unaffected.**
- **Appear enthusiastic, yet not effusive.**
- **Appear pleasant, yet serious.**
- **Appear confident, yet not arrogant.**

Above all, your listeners expect you to remain in control. They're extremely sensitive to any kind of negative behavior. They can't help you through your performance, so they tend to become uncomfortable and even embarrassed when you appear to be in trouble. *Thus, regardless of how you think your performance is going, you must never appear disgusted, disappointed, or display any other negative feelings.*

Finally, your general appearance is an important consideration. You should dress in a manner which doesn't distract the audience. Preferably, you should wear whatever is commonly accepted for the type of performance you're presenting — formal attire for a formal performance, informal attire for an informal performance. Personal grooming is also important. Conservative taste in hair styling and general neatness implies a refinement in your approach to performing. Indeed, sensitivity to your general appearance also reflects your sensitivity as an artist.

Carrying the Guitar

You should carry the guitar in a manner which appears graceful and provides maximum convenience and control. To accomplish this, you need to grasp the guitar properly.

With the guitar in conventional playing position, grasp the neck near the guitar body with your right hand. Notice how easily you can move the guitar into and out of playing position. Acquire the habit of grasping the guitar this way whenever carrying or removing it from its case.

Guidelines for Walking to the Chair

The way you walk onstage can convey either confidence and enthusiasm or uncertainty and indifference. To convey a positive spirit to the audience, smile pleasantly as you walk briskly and purposefully to the chair. Carry the guitar almost vertically. Walk to a point in front of the chair (to the right of the footstand) which allows you to be seated without taking an additional step.

If you have a choice, always enter from the right of the chair. If you must enter from the left, walk around the rear of the chair to avoid turning your back to the audience. Never walk to the left of the footstand — this requires you to step over the footstand before being seated. Such a maneuver looks awkward and poses the risk of accidently tripping over the footstand.

Keep your eyes on the chair or a short distance ahead of where you're walking — you should pause to face the audience only after you've reached the proper position in front of the chair. On arriving in front of the chair, stand with your feet somewhat close together. *Until you're an accomplished performer, avoid eye contact with the audience by looking at a point just above and beyond their heads.*

Guidelines for Bowing

Bowing is always in response to applause. If there's applause as you walk onstage, you should acknowledge it with a definite but somewhat reserved nod. Without hesitation, sit and position the guitar for playing. The thought here is that, since you haven't yet given the audience anything to applaud, their applause is a polite greeting and the program should begin without delay.

A crucial point is reached when you've finished playing a piece or a group of pieces. You should clearly indicate this finish with a definite gesture. As you play the last note or chord of the piece, make a free outward flourish with your right hand. Then, as you stop the strings with your right hand (or when the last note has died away), move your left hand to the juncture of the guitar body and neck. Look up and smile discreetly, thus signaling that applause is appropriate.

Most people understand that applause isn't appropriate when the performer is looking down. Some performers are apparently unaware of this — on concluding a piece, they neither look up nor change expression. This sometimes creates a long and embarrassing silence before the audience realizes that applause is appropriate. The responsibility to avoid this is solely yours.

Again, bowing is only in response to applause. You should give no indication of rising before the audience begins to applaud. Occasionally, poorly trained guitarists will end a piece with a flair and jump to their feet in anticipation of applause. This shows a definite lack of discretion and control. Once applause begins, however, your response should be prompt and spirited. Again, poorly trained guitarists sometimes convey a lack of appreciation by remaining seated during applause. Except between movements or a programmed selection of pieces, failure to stand and bow in response to applause is an act of rudeness to the audience.

Acquiring the ability to stand and bow gracefully requires well-directed thought and practice:

❑ **With your right hand, grasp the neck of the guitar close to the body.**

❑ **As you lift the guitar off your left thigh, place your left foot to the right of the footstand.**

❑ **The guitar should now be almost vertical and momentarily balanced on your right thigh. As you begin to stand, slide the guitar to the right — this brings the guitar off your thigh and allows you to stand easily and naturally.**

❑ **In preparation for bowing, bring your right foot forward so that it's even with your left. Hold the guitar somewhat to the right as you bow.**

Guitarists sometimes attempt to stand with their foot still on the footstand. This is quite a balancing act to behold! Occasionally the footstand crashes over and bedlam prevails.

Different degrees of applause demand different bows in response. Although this isn't necessarily a consideration in a DP, you should know how to respond in different situations. Enthusiastic, prolonged applause demands a somewhat deeper and prolonged bow, perhaps more than one bow in succession. More reserved applause requires more discreet bowing, or perhaps a courteous nod. To avoid appearing pompous, keep the depth and time of your bow somewhat conservative. It's better to be seated (or spiritedly exit, as the case may be) promptly. If the applause continues, stand or reappear and bow again. Never wait for the applause to subside before exiting or being seated.

Bear in mind that, until you can carry it out by habit, effective stage conduct will feel somewhat awkward. But with sufficient practice, applying these concepts will increase your confidence during any performance situation.

Practicing a Formal DP

Now you're ready to begin practicing a formal DP, including proper stage conduct, in the privacy of your practice room. Again, imagine that you're playing for a large audience. Your aim should be to become comfortable and secure with this procedure:

- **briskly walking to the chair**
- **bowing gracefully to acknowledge imaginary applause**
- **being seated, positioning the guitar, and tuning**
- **playing**
- **standing and bowing, again to acknowledge imaginary applause**
- **spiritedly walking "offstage"**

Practice this procedure over a period of time, until you can carry it out by habit — only then will you gain the confidence to freely share the warmth of your personality with the audience.

Next, perform for one or more persons. Ask them to behave and applaud as though they're attending a formal recital. After each session, invite your listeners to comment on all aspects of your performance, including your conduct before and after playing.

When you feel confident with this procedure, you should begin forming another extremely important habit. Your entire performance can be affected by how you approach the few minutes before you walk onstage. A positive beginning tends to set the course for what follows. Thus, *before walking onstage,* you should do the following:

❑ **Breathe slowly and deeply several times. Visualize as clearly as possible the beginning and successive phrases of your first piece.**

❑ **In your mind's eye, see yourself performing the first piece. In your mind's ear, hear the music unfolding at the correct tempo.**

Slow, deep breathing helps control excitement — you should continue this as you walk to the chair. Clear visualization induces confidence and the correct focus of concentration.

Remember, the purpose of a DP is to develop your ability to concentrate sufficiently to play with acceptable accuracy and confidence. Don't judge yourself by accuracy alone — also evaluate how you felt before, during, and after a performance. If you had negative feelings during a performance, you haven't yet achieved the aim of a DP, even though you may have played with acceptable accuracy. Approach each performance with sincere appreciation for the privilege of being able to share music with others.

The Expressive Performance (EP)

An EP is the last step before an actual recital. In fact, the only difference between an EP and a formal recital is the audience: The audience of an EP is composed of students who share a similar interest in learning to perform — a formal recital is intended for the general public. You should practice an EP in preparation for any formal recital.

The prime requirement for an EP is continuity. Once you begin playing, you must play the entire piece without hesitations. Although an occasional missed note is undesirable, it won't be a significant distraction to either you or your listeners if you continue to play without hesitation. If you can't perform a piece with continuity, you haven't sufficiently prepared for an EP.

It's essential to clearly understand how an EP differs from a DP:

- **In a DP, you emphasize your development as a performer. Both a slower-than-normal tempo and an occasional deliberate pause are permitted.**

- **In an EP, you've presumably reached a stage where you can play the music at a satisfactory tempo during a performance situation. You're now emphasizing musical expression. You should strive to ignore any minor errors in your playing — instead, concentrate only on playing the music expressively.**

Summary

The concepts behind learning to perform aren't complex. There are certain things you can think about which will help you to concentrate securely and confidently. There are other things you can think about which will hinder your ability to concentrate. Thus, learning to perform means learning to concentrate on positive considerations and avoiding negative considerations. Always strive to concentrate on the positive performance concerns, and consistently discipline yourself to form a positive, friendly, and appreciative attitude toward your audience.

Always remember, however, that performance development isn't an isolated aspect of study. You'll perform only as well as you approach your overall study and practice. *If you're insecure in one area of your development, you'll inevitably be an insecure performer — thus, you must strive for security and confidence in every area of guitar study.*

Applying these concepts takes time, especially if you have a background of severe performance anxiety. But it can be done. Like every other area of guitar study, performance development is a matter of acquiring correct habits. With patience and careful study, you can learn to share music with security and confidence.